I0110556

VOILA!
JOURNAL FOR COOKS

Activinotes

Activinotes
DAILY JOURNALS, PLANNERS, NOTEBOOKS AND OTHER BLANK BOOKS

Copyright 2016

All Rights reserved. No part of this book may be reproduced or used in any way or form or by any means whether electronic or mechanical, this means that you cannot record or photocopy any material ideas or tips that are provided in this book.

This Book Belongs To

_____

Recipe Index

Name	Reference	Page

Recipe Index

Name	Reference	Page

Name:

Recipes

Ingredients:

_____

_____

_____

_____

_____

_____

Instructions:

_____

_____

_____

_____

_____

_____

Notes:

_____

_____

_____

_____

_____

_____

Name:

Recipes

Ingredients:

_____
_____
_____
_____
_____
_____

Instructions:

_____
_____
_____
_____
_____
_____

Notes:

_____
_____
_____
_____
_____
_____

Name:

Recipes

Ingredients:

_____

_____

_____

_____

_____

_____

_____

Instructions:

_____

_____

_____

_____

_____

_____

_____

Notes:

_____

_____

_____

_____

_____

_____

Name:

Recipes

Ingredients:

_____
_____
_____
_____
_____
_____

Instructions:

_____
_____
_____
_____
_____
_____

Notes:

_____
_____
_____
_____
_____
_____

Name:

Recipes

Ingredients:

_____

_____

_____

_____

_____

_____

Instructions:

_____

_____

_____

_____

_____

_____

Notes:

_____

_____

_____

_____

_____

_____

Name:

Recipes

Ingredients:

_____

_____

_____

_____

_____

_____

_____

Instructions:

_____

_____

_____

_____

_____

_____

Notes:

_____

_____

_____

_____

_____

_____

Name:

Recipes

Ingredients:

_____

_____

_____

_____

_____

_____

_____

Instructions:

_____

_____

_____

_____

_____

_____

_____

Notes:

_____

_____

_____

_____

_____

_____

Name:

Recipes

Ingredients:

_____
_____
_____
_____
_____
_____

Instructions:

_____
_____
_____
_____
_____
_____

Notes:

_____
_____
_____
_____
_____
_____

Name:

Ingredients:

_____

_____

_____

_____

_____

_____

Instructions:

_____

_____

_____

_____

_____

_____

Notes:

_____

_____

_____

_____

_____

_____

Recipes

Name:

Recipes

Ingredients:

_____

_____

_____

_____

_____

_____

Instructions:

_____

_____

_____

_____

_____

_____

Notes:

_____

_____

_____

_____

_____

_____

Name:

Recipes

Ingredients:

_____

_____

_____

_____

_____

_____

Instructions:

_____

_____

_____

_____

_____

_____

_____

Notes:

_____

_____

_____

_____

_____

_____

Name:

Recipes

Ingredients:

_____

_____

_____

_____

_____

_____

_____

Instructions:

_____

_____

_____

_____

_____

_____

_____

Notes:

_____

_____

_____

_____

_____

_____

Name:

Recipes

Ingredients:

_____

_____

_____

_____

_____

_____

Instructions:

_____

_____

_____

_____

_____

_____

Notes:

_____

_____

_____

_____

_____

_____

Name:

Recipes

Ingredients:

_____

_____

_____

_____

_____

_____

Instructions:

_____

_____

_____

_____

_____

_____

Notes:

_____

_____

_____

_____

_____

_____

Name:

Recipes

Ingredients:

_____

_____

_____

_____

_____

_____

_____

Instructions:

_____

_____

_____

_____

_____

_____

Notes:

_____

_____

_____

_____

_____

_____

Name:

Recipes

Ingredients:

_____
_____
_____
_____
_____
_____
_____

Instructions:

_____
_____
_____
_____
_____
_____
_____

Notes:

_____
_____
_____
_____
_____
_____
_____

Name:

Ingredients:

Recipes

Instructions:

Notes:

Name:

Recipes

Ingredients:

_____

_____

_____

_____

_____

_____

_____

Instructions:

_____

_____

_____

_____

_____

_____

Notes:

_____

_____

_____

_____

_____

_____

Name:

Recipes

Ingredients:

_____

_____

_____

_____

_____

_____

Instructions:

_____

_____

_____

_____

_____

_____

Notes:

_____

_____

_____

_____

_____

_____

Name:

Recipes

Ingredients:

_____

_____

_____

_____

_____

_____

Instructions:

_____

_____

_____

_____

_____

_____

Notes:

_____

_____

_____

_____

_____

_____

Name:

Ingredients:

Recipes

_____

_____

_____

_____

_____

Instructions:

_____

_____

_____

_____

_____

_____

Notes:

_____

_____

_____

_____

_____

_____

Name:

Recipes

Ingredients:

_____

_____

_____

_____

_____

_____

Instructions:

_____

_____

_____

_____

_____

_____

Notes:

_____

_____

_____

_____

_____

Name:

Recipes

Ingredients:

_____

_____

_____

_____

_____

_____

Instructions:

_____

_____

_____

_____

_____

_____

Notes:

_____

_____

_____

_____

_____

_____

Name:

Recipes

Ingredients:

_____

_____

_____

_____

_____

_____

Instructions:

_____

_____

_____

_____

_____

_____

Notes:

_____

_____

_____

_____

_____

_____

Name:

Recipes

Ingredients:

_____
_____
_____
_____
_____
_____
_____

Instructions:

_____
_____
_____
_____
_____
_____
_____

Notes:

_____
_____
_____
_____
_____
_____
_____

Name:

Recipes

Ingredients:

_____

_____

_____

_____

_____

_____

_____

Instructions:

_____

_____

_____

_____

_____

_____

_____

Notes:

_____

_____

_____

_____

_____

_____

Name:

Recipes

Ingredients:

_____

_____

_____

_____

_____

_____

Instructions:

_____

_____

_____

_____

_____

_____

Notes:

_____

_____

_____

_____

_____

Name:

Recipes

Ingredients:

_____

_____

_____

_____

_____

_____

Instructions:

_____

_____

_____

_____

_____

_____

Notes:

_____

_____

_____

_____

_____

_____

Name:

Ingredients:

Recipes

_____

_____

_____

_____

_____

_____

Instructions:

_____

_____

_____

_____

_____

_____

Notes:

_____

_____

_____

_____

_____

_____

Name:

Recipes

Ingredients:

_____
_____
_____
_____
_____
_____

Instructions:

_____
_____
_____
_____
_____
_____

Notes:

_____
_____
_____
_____
_____

Name:

Recipes

Ingredients:

_____

_____

_____

_____

_____

_____

Instructions:

_____

_____

_____

_____

_____

Notes:

_____

_____

_____

_____

_____

_____

Name:

Recipes

Ingredients:

_____
_____
_____
_____
_____
_____

Instructions:

_____
_____
_____
_____
_____
_____
_____

Notes:

_____
_____
_____
_____
_____
_____

Name:

Recipes

Ingredients:

_____

_____

_____

_____

_____

_____

Instructions:

_____

_____

_____

_____

_____

_____

Notes:

_____

_____

_____

_____

_____

_____

Name:

Ingredients:

_____

_____

_____

_____

_____

_____

Instructions:

_____

_____

_____

_____

_____

_____

Notes:

_____

_____

_____

_____

_____

_____

Recipes

Name:

Recipes

Ingredients:

_____
_____
_____
_____
_____
_____

Instructions:

_____
_____
_____
_____
_____
_____

Notes:

_____
_____
_____
_____
_____
_____

Name:

Recipes

Ingredients:

_____

_____

_____

_____

_____

_____

Instructions:

_____

_____

_____

_____

_____

_____

Notes:

_____

_____

_____

_____

_____

_____

Name:

Recipes

Ingredients:

_____

_____

_____

_____

_____

_____

Instructions:

_____

_____

_____

_____

_____

_____

Notes:

_____

_____

_____

_____

_____

_____

Name:

Recipes

Ingredients:

_____

_____

_____

_____

_____

_____

Instructions:

_____

_____

_____

_____

_____

_____

Notes:

_____

_____

_____

_____

_____

_____

Name:

Recipes

Ingredients:

_____

_____

_____

_____

_____

_____

_____

Instructions:

_____

_____

_____

_____

_____

_____

_____

Notes:

_____

_____

_____

_____

_____

_____

Name:

Recipes

Ingredients:

_____

_____

_____

_____

_____

_____

_____

Instructions:

_____

_____

_____

_____

_____

_____

Notes:

_____

_____

_____

_____

_____

_____

Name:

Recipes

Ingredients:

_____
_____
_____
_____
_____
_____
_____

Instructions:

_____
_____
_____
_____
_____
_____
_____

Notes:

_____
_____
_____
_____
_____
_____

Name:

Recipes

Ingredients:

_____
_____
_____
_____
_____
_____
_____

Instructions:

_____
_____
_____
_____
_____
_____

Notes:

_____
_____
_____
_____
_____
_____

Name:

Recipes

Ingredients:

_____
_____
_____
_____
_____
_____

Instructions:

_____
_____
_____
_____
_____
_____

Notes:

_____
_____
_____
_____
_____
_____

Name:

Recipes

Ingredients:

_____

_____

_____

_____

_____

_____

Instructions:

_____

_____

_____

_____

_____

_____

Notes:

_____

_____

_____

_____

_____

_____

Name:

Recipes

Ingredients:

_____
_____
_____
_____
_____
_____

Instructions:

_____
_____
_____
_____
_____
_____

Notes:

_____
_____
_____
_____
_____

Name:

Recipes

Ingredients:

_____

_____

_____

_____

_____

_____

Instructions:

_____

_____

_____

_____

_____

_____

Notes:

_____

_____

_____

_____

_____

_____

_____

Name:

Ingredients:

_____
_____
_____
_____
_____
_____

Instructions:

_____
_____
_____
_____
_____
_____

Notes:

_____
_____
_____
_____
_____
_____

Recipes

Name:

Recipes

Ingredients:

_____

_____

_____

_____

_____

_____

Instructions:

_____

_____

_____

_____

_____

_____

Notes:

_____

_____

_____

_____

_____

Name:

Recipes

Ingredients:

_____
_____
_____
_____
_____
_____

Instructions:

_____
_____
_____
_____
_____
_____

Notes:

_____
_____
_____
_____
_____
_____
_____

Name:

Recipes

Ingredients:

_____

_____

_____

_____

_____

_____

Instructions:

_____

_____

_____

_____

_____

_____

Notes:

_____

_____

_____

_____

_____

Name:

Recipes

Ingredients:

_____
_____
_____
_____
_____
_____
_____

Instructions:

_____
_____
_____
_____
_____
_____

Notes:

_____
_____
_____
_____
_____
_____

Name:

Recipes

Ingredients:

_____

_____

_____

_____

_____

_____

Instructions:

_____

_____

_____

_____

_____

_____

_____

Notes:

_____

_____

_____

_____

_____

_____

Name:

Recipes

Ingredients:

_____

_____

_____

_____

_____

_____

Instructions:

_____

_____

_____

_____

_____

_____

Notes:

_____

_____

_____

_____

_____

_____

Name:

Recipes

Ingredients:

_____
_____
_____
_____
_____
_____
_____

Instructions:

_____
_____
_____
_____
_____
_____
_____

Notes:

_____
_____
_____
_____
_____
_____

Name:

Recipes

Ingredients:

_____
_____
_____
_____
_____
_____

Instructions:

_____
_____
_____
_____
_____
_____

Notes:

_____
_____
_____
_____
_____
_____

Name:

Recipes

Ingredients:

_____

_____

_____

_____

_____

_____

_____

Instructions:

_____

_____

_____

_____

_____

_____

_____

Notes:

_____

_____

_____

_____

_____

_____

Name:

Recipes

Ingredients:

_____

_____

_____

_____

_____

_____

Instructions:

_____

_____

_____

_____

_____

_____

Notes:

_____

_____

_____

_____

_____

_____

Name:

Recipes

Ingredients:

_____

_____

_____

_____

_____

_____

Instructions:

_____

_____

_____

_____

_____

_____

Notes:

_____

_____

_____

_____

_____

_____

Name:

Recipes

Ingredients:

_____

_____

_____

_____

_____

_____

_____

Instructions:

_____

_____

_____

_____

_____

_____

Notes:

_____

_____

_____

_____

_____

_____

Name:

Ingredients:
_____
_____
_____
_____
_____
_____

Instructions:
_____
_____
_____
_____
_____
_____

Notes:
_____
_____
_____
_____
_____

Recipes

Name:

Recipes

Ingredients:

_____

_____

_____

_____

_____

_____

Instructions:

_____

_____

_____

_____

_____

_____

Notes:

_____

_____

_____

_____

_____

_____

Name:

Recipes

Ingredients:

_____
_____
_____
_____
_____
_____

Instructions:

_____
_____
_____
_____
_____
_____

Notes:

_____
_____
_____
_____
_____
_____

Name:

Recipes

Ingredients:

_____
_____
_____
_____
_____
_____

Instructions:

_____
_____
_____
_____
_____
_____

Notes:

_____
_____
_____
_____
_____
_____

Name:

Recipes

Ingredients:

_____

_____

_____

_____

_____

_____

Instructions:

_____

_____

_____

_____

_____

_____

Notes:

_____

_____

_____

_____

_____

_____

Name:

Recipes

Ingredients:

_____

_____

_____

_____

_____

_____

Instructions:

_____

_____

_____

_____

_____

_____

Notes:

_____

_____

_____

_____

_____

Name:

Recipes

Ingredients:

_____

_____

_____

_____

_____

_____

Instructions:

_____

_____

_____

_____

_____

_____

Notes:

_____

_____

_____

_____

_____

_____

Name:

Recipes

Ingredients:

_____

_____

_____

_____

_____

_____

_____

Instructions:

_____

_____

_____

_____

_____

_____

_____

Notes:

_____

_____

_____

_____

_____

_____

Name:

Recipes

Ingredients:

_____

_____

_____

_____

_____

_____

Instructions:

_____

_____

_____

_____

_____

_____

Notes:

_____

_____

_____

_____

_____

Name:

Recipes

Ingredients:

_____

_____

_____

_____

_____

_____

Instructions:

_____

_____

_____

_____

_____

_____

_____

Notes:

_____

_____

_____

_____

_____

_____

Name:

Recipes

Ingredients:

_____

_____

_____

_____

_____

_____

_____

Instructions:

_____

_____

_____

_____

_____

_____

Notes:

_____

_____

_____

_____

_____

_____

Name:

Recipes

Ingredients:

_____

_____

_____

_____

_____

_____

Instructions:

_____

_____

_____

_____

_____

_____

Notes:

_____

_____

_____

_____

_____

_____

Name:

Recipes

Ingredients:

_____

_____

_____

_____

_____

_____

Instructions:

_____

_____

_____

_____

_____

_____

Notes:

_____

_____

_____

_____

_____

Name:

Recipes

Ingredients:

_____
_____
_____
_____
_____
_____
_____

Instructions:

_____
_____
_____
_____
_____
_____
_____

Notes:

_____
_____
_____
_____
_____
_____

Name:

Recipes

Ingredients:

_____

_____

_____

_____

_____

_____

Instructions:

_____

_____

_____

_____

_____

_____

Notes:

_____

_____

_____

_____

_____

_____

Name:

Recipes

Ingredients:

_____
_____
_____
_____
_____
_____

Instructions:

_____
_____
_____
_____
_____
_____

Notes:

_____
_____
_____
_____
_____

Name:

Recipes

Ingredients:

_____

_____

_____

_____

_____

_____

Instructions:

_____

_____

_____

_____

_____

_____

Notes:

_____

_____

_____

_____

_____

_____

Name:

Recipes

Ingredients:

_____

_____

_____

_____

_____

_____

_____

Instructions:

_____

_____

_____

_____

_____

_____

_____

Notes:

_____

_____

_____

_____

_____

_____

Name:

Recipes

Ingredients:

_____
_____
_____
_____
_____
_____

Instructions:

_____
_____
_____
_____
_____
_____

Notes:

_____
_____
_____
_____
_____
_____

Name:

Recipes

Ingredients:

_____

_____

_____

_____

_____

_____

Instructions:

_____

_____

_____

_____

_____

Notes:

_____

_____

_____

_____

_____

Name:

Recipes

Ingredients:

_____
_____
_____
_____
_____
_____

Instructions:

_____
_____
_____
_____
_____
_____
_____

Notes:

_____
_____
_____
_____
_____
_____

Name:

Recipes

Ingredients:

_____

_____

_____

_____

_____

_____

Instructions:

_____

_____

_____

_____

_____

_____

Notes:

_____

_____

_____

_____

_____

_____

Name:

Recipes

Ingredients:

_____

_____

_____

_____

_____

_____

Instructions:

_____

_____

_____

_____

_____

_____

Notes:

_____

_____

_____

_____

_____

_____

Name:

Recipes

Ingredients:

_____

_____

_____

_____

_____

_____

_____

Instructions:

_____

_____

_____

_____

_____

_____

_____

Notes:

_____

_____

_____

_____

_____

_____

Name:

Recipes

Ingredients:

_____

_____

_____

_____

_____

_____

Instructions:

_____

_____

_____

_____

_____

_____

Notes:

_____

_____

_____

_____

_____

_____

Name:

Recipes

Ingredients:

_____
_____
_____
_____
_____
_____

Instructions:

_____
_____
_____
_____
_____
_____

Notes:

_____
_____
_____
_____
_____

Name:

Recipes

Ingredients:

_____

_____

_____

_____

_____

_____

Instructions:

_____

_____

_____

_____

_____

_____

Notes:

_____

_____

_____

_____

_____

Name:

Recipes

Ingredients:

_____
_____
_____
_____
_____
_____
_____

Instructions:

_____
_____
_____
_____
_____
_____
_____

Notes:

_____
_____
_____
_____
_____
_____
_____

Name:

Recipes

Ingredients:

_____
_____
_____
_____
_____
_____

Instructions:

_____
_____
_____
_____
_____
_____

Notes:

_____
_____
_____
_____
_____
_____

Name:

Recipes

Ingredients:

_____
_____
_____
_____
_____
_____

Instructions:

_____
_____
_____
_____
_____
_____

Notes:

_____
_____
_____
_____
_____
_____

Name:

Recipes

Ingredients:

_____

_____

_____

_____

_____

_____

Instructions:

_____

_____

_____

_____

_____

_____

Notes:

_____

_____

_____

_____

_____

_____

Name:

Recipes

Ingredients:

_____
_____
_____
_____
_____
_____
_____

Instructions:

_____
_____
_____
_____
_____
_____
_____

Notes:

_____
_____
_____
_____
_____
_____
_____

Name:

Recipes

Ingredients:
_____
_____
_____
_____
_____
_____

Instructions:
_____
_____
_____
_____
_____
_____

Notes:
_____
_____
_____
_____
_____
_____

Name:

Recipes

Ingredients:

_____

_____

_____

_____

_____

_____

Instructions:

_____

_____

_____

_____

_____

_____

Notes:

_____

_____

_____

_____

_____

_____

www.ingramcontent.com/pod-product-compliance
Lightning Source LLC
Chambersburg PA
CBHW081338090426

42737CB00017B/3200

9781683218821